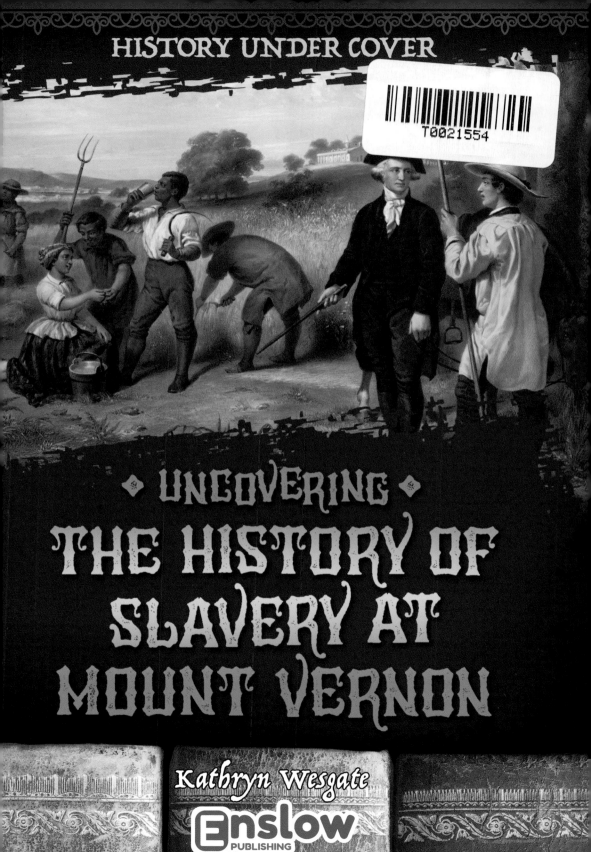

T0021554

UNCOVERING
THE HISTORY OF SLAVERY AT MOUNT VERNON

Kathryn Wesgate

Enslow
PUBLISHING

Please visit our website, www.enslow.com. For a free color catalog of all our high-quality books, call toll free 1-800-398-2504 or fax 1-877-980-4454.

Library of Congress Cataloging-in-Publication Data

Names: Wesgate, Kathryn, author.
Title: Uncovering the history of slavery at Mount Vernon / Kathryn Wesgate.
Other titles: History under cover.
Description: New York : Enslow Publishing, [2023] | Series: History under cover | Includes index.
Identifiers: LCCN 2021055349 | ISBN 9781978528918 (set) | ISBN 9781978528925 (library binding) | ISBN 9781978528901 (paperback) | ISBN 9781978528932 (ebook)
Subjects: LCSH: Washington, George, 1732-1799–Juvenile literature. | Slaves–Virginia–Mount Vernon (Estate)–Juvenile literature. | Slavery–Virginia–Mount Vernon (Estate)–Juvenile literature. | Mount Vernon (Va. : Estate)–History–18th century–Juvenile literature. | Mount Vernon (Va. : Estate)–Antiquities–Juvenile literature.
Classification: LCC E312.5 .W47 2023 | DDC 306.3/62097341–dc23/eng/20211123
LC record available at https://lccn.loc.gov/2021055349

Published in 2023 by
Enslow Publishing
29 East 21st Street
New York, NY 10010

Copyright © 2023 Enslow Publishing

Portions of this work were originally authored by Janey Levy and published as *Slavery at Mount Vernon*. All new material this edition authored by Kathryn Wesgate.

Designer: Leslie Taylor
Editor: Kate Mikoley

Photo credits: Photo credits: series art (scrolls) Magenta10/Shutterstock.com, series art (back cover leather texture) levan828/Shutterstock.com; series art (front cover books) RMMPPhotography/Shutterstock.com; series art (title font) MagicPics/Shutterstock.com; series art (ripped inside pgs) kaczor58/Shutterstock.com; p. 4 Everett Collection/Shutterstock.com; p. 5 (map) https://www.loc.gov/item/2009582413/; p. 5 (top) Bob Pool/Shutterstock.com; p. 6 (and cover image) Everett Collection/Shutterstock.com; p. 7 (cabin interior) https://commons.wikimedia.org/wiki/File:Slave_Cabin_interior_02_-_Mount_Vernon.jpg; p. 7 John M. Chase/Shutterstock.com; p. 8 https://commons.wikimedia.org/wiki/File:The_Marquis_de_Lafayette_MET_DT2057.jpg; p. 9 https://commons.wikimedia.org/wiki/File:The_First_Meeting_of_Washington_and_Lafayette—Philadelphia,_August_3rd,_1777_MET_DP853568.jpg; p. 10 World History Archive/Alamy.com; p. 11 North Wind Picture Archives/Alamy.com; p. 12 Everett Collection/Shutterstock.com; p. 13 https://commons.wikimedia.org/wiki/File:Gilbert_Stuart_-_Portrait_of_George_Washington%27s_CookFXD.jpg; p. 14 Asar Studios/Alamy.com; p. 15 Jim Engelbrecht_DanitaDelimont.com/Alamy.com; p. 14 Tony Campbell/Shutterstock.com; p. 16 https://commons.wikimedia.org/wiki/File:Slave_Cabin_interior_04_-_Mount_Vernon.jpg; p. 17 Jacquelyn Martin/APImages.com; p. 18 Peter Newark American Pictures/Bridgemanimages.com; p. 19 North Wind Picture Archives/Alamy.com; p. 20 https://commons.wikimedia.org/wiki/File:Slave_Cabin_chicken_coop_-_Mount_Vernon.jpg; p. 21 Brenda Kean/Alamy.com; p. 22 Bokeh_pho/Shutterstock.com; p. 23 Pictures Now/Alamy.com; p. 23_inset Detroit Publishing Co./LOC.com; p. 24 Pictures from History/Bridgemanimages.com; p. 25 North Wind Picture Archives/Alamy.com; p. 27 https://commons.wikimedia.org/wiki/File:Gen._George_Washington_and_his_family._(Geo._Washington_Parke_Custis,_Gen._George_Washington,_Eleanore_Parke_Custis,_Martha_Washington,_William_Lee)_(NYPL_Hades-254222-EM13214).jpg; p. 28 https://commons.wikimedia.org/wiki/File:Slave_Memorial_-_detail_-_Mount_Vernon.jpg; p. 29 https://commons.wikimedia.org/wiki/File:Mount_Vernon_Slave_Memorial.jpg.

Printed in the United States of America

Some of the images in this book illustrate individuals who are models. The depictions do not imply actual situations or events.

CPSIA compliance information: Batch #CSENS23: For further information, contact Enslow Publishing, New York, New York, at 1-800-398-2504.

Find us on 🅕 🅞

Contents

Words in the glossary appear in bold or highlighted type the first time they are used in the text.

Founding Father and Enslaver

Mount Vernon's House for Families was one of the main **quarters** for enslaved people at George Washington's residence, the Mansion House Farm. Between 1984 and 1991, archaeologists excavated the site where the structure once stood. Their findings shed new light on the lives of those enslaved there.

The **artifacts** uncovered—including glass, tobacco pipes, and table **utensils**—suggested those enslaved at Mount Vernon may have received material benefits from living so near the Washington family. Yet the fact remains that these people were enslaved.

Mount Vernon holds a special place in U.S. history, but its story of slavery has remained largely hidden until recently. It can be difficult to accept the **contradiction** of a Founding Father who fought for liberty but himself was an enslaver. Read on to learn more about George Washington's role in slavery and its history at Mount Vernon.

George Washington

The mansion (above) is the building most people picture when they think of Mount Vernon.

~ More About the Estate ~

Mount Vernon was divided into five separate farms: Mansion House Farm, Dogue Run Farm, River Farm, Muddy Hole Farm, and Union Farm. The largest, Mansion House Farm, was centered around the mansion, Washington's stately home shown in images of Mount Vernon. Washington's father built a small house at the site in 1735. George's brother Lawrence added to it after it became his in 1743. George enlarged it even more after Lawrence's death. Archaeologists believe some of the artifacts uncovered at the House for Families were probably handed down from the Washingtons to the people they enslaved.

Washington's Enslaved Workers

It's not news that Washington enslaved people. Many **documents** provide evidence of it. However, the subject hasn't received much public attention until recently. Now, more people recognize the importance of discussing slavery at Mount Vernon and Washington's attitude toward it.

Washington grew up in a society that treated slavery as a normal part of life. Many white people in America viewed enslaved Black people as property to be bought and sold. Washington shared this view for most of his life. He was only 11 when his father died and 10 people his father enslaved became his property. As a young adult, he purchased and enslaved at least eight more people. In 1755, he bought seven more, including a child. In 1759, Washington's marriage to the widow Martha Dandridge Custis brought 84 more enslaved people to Mount Vernon.

Washington on his farm with enslaved workers

This cabin is a recreation of the type of building many enslaved people likely lived in at Mount Vernon. Made with wood and mud, these cabins were often leaky and poorly made.

~ From the Outside Looking In ~

In 1798, a Polish visitor spent 12 days at Mount Vernon. He wrote about Washington and the people he enslaved, stating, "General Washington treats his slaves far more humanely [compassionately] than do his fellow citizens of Virginia." However, the man also wrote that the people who were enslaved worked nearly nonstop. Of their living conditions he said, "We entered one of the huts of the Blacks, for one cannot call them by the name of houses. They are more miserable than the most miserable of the cottages of our peasants."

Washington commonly separated the men and women he enslaved. This meant husbands and wives were forced to live apart from each other. Skilled males were housed close to the mansion, while their wives and children were on the outer farms. About 65 percent of the enslaved field workers were women. Washington approved of harsh punishments, which he called corrections, for even minor offenses.

The American Revolution changed Washington's views on slavery. He witnessed the courage of Black soldiers fighting in the Continental army. He was also exposed to the antislavery views of the Marquis de Lafayette, a wealthy French nobleman who came to

Marquis de Lafayette

America to support the colonies during the Revolution. While Washington never publicly supported the abolition of slavery, he hoped Congress would end it. However, he continued enslaving people.

The Marquis de Lafayette strongly supported the right of people to rule themselves and firmly opposed slavery. He and Washington became close friends.

PUBLISHED BY CURRIER & IVES.   Copyright 1876. by Currier & Ives. N.Y.   129 NASSAU ST. NEW YORK.

THE FIRST MEETING OF WASHINGTON AND LAFAYETTE.
Philadelphia, August 3rd 1777.

~ Washington's Will ~

Though he enslaved many, Washington's will directed that they all be freed after his wife's death. In it, he wrote: "Upon the decease [death] of my wife, it is my Will & desire that all the Slaves which I hold in my own right, shall receive their freedom." However, only 123 of the 317 people then enslaved at Mount Vernon were considered his. Most of the others were Martha's and legally belonged to her first husband's estate. Neither George nor Martha had the right to free them. They would return to the Custis family after Martha's death.

9

Tough Labor

Being enslaved at Mount Vernon usually involved working from sunrise to sunset, with about two hours off for meals. That meant those who were enslaved worked about eight hours a day during the winter, when there are fewer hours of daylight. During the summer, when days are longer, they might work as many as 14 hours a day.

Enslaved workers at Mount Vernon labored six days a week, with Sundays off. They also received a few holidays a year. However, when a job such as harvesting had to be completed within a limited time, they had to work through their days off. In these

situations, once the job was finished, they might receive money or another day off to make up for time off they missed— although this, of course, was not promised.

When enslaved people had children, they too were enslaved. Young children were not able to work as hard as adults could. However, enslaved children often had jobs too, such as cleaning or caring for younger children.

~ Many Kinds of Work ~

According to a list of enslaved people at Mount Vernon put together in 1799, about 42 percent of those enslaved there were either too young or too old to work. There were also some whose physical abilities didn't allow them to do very hard, demanding labor. These people were often given jobs such as making clothing or shoes or picking wild onion seeds out of the store of oat seeds. Most of the enslaved laborers who could do hard work worked in the fields.

Mount Vernon

Of the people enslaved at Mount Vernon who were able to work, slightly more than a quarter were skilled laborers. These people worked as servants, blacksmiths, barrel makers, cooks, dairymaids, **distillers**, gardeners, millers, **seamstresses**, shoemakers, spinners, knitters, ditch diggers, wagon drivers, or carriage drivers. They were housed close to the mansion. Almost 75 percent of these workers were men.

Nearly three-quarters of the enslaved workers worked in the fields. Most of these field workers were women. The work was hard, demanding physical labor, which included plowing and harvesting. They also collected and spread manure, pulled tree stumps out of the ground, and built fences around Mount Vernon.

Work at the mansion was often preferred to work in the fields. Washington sometimes threatened to punish enslaved house workers by sending them to the fields.

This portrait is thought to be of Washington's cook, Hercules. While enslaved people all had difficult lives, those at Mount Vernon often preferred jobs inside to those that involved working in the fields.

~ Washington's Household Staff ~

Of the people they enslaved, wealthy enslavers often preferred to have lighter-skinned people work inside the house. Washington preferred this as well. Many of the individuals that made up Washington's household staff were of mixed ancestry. In their case, this meant a parent, or perhaps a grandparent, had been a white person. This was something that visitors of the Washingtons often noted. One visitor wrote of meeting a boy with such fair hair and skin color "that if I had not been told, I should never have suspected his [African] ancestry."

Housing

The House for Families can be seen in this painting from the late 1700s.

House for Families

The House for Families mentioned earlier in this book was the quarters for enslaved people who worked in the mansion and skilled workers on the Mansion House Farm. It was a two-story wooden building with a brick foundation, a **chimney** at each end, and glass windows. As far as quality of construction, it was nicer than most of the other slave quarters at Mount Vernon. However, the people living there had little privacy from each other and from their enslaver.

The House for Families was torn down in the 1790s. Beginning around 1793, most of the people enslaved at the Mansion House Farm lived in brick wings off the greenhouse. The wings contained a total of four large rooms, each with a fireplace, built-in beds, and glass windows. These wings also didn't offer much privacy.

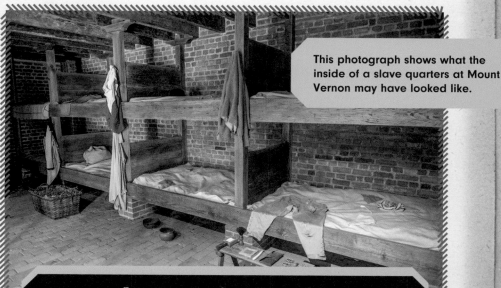

This photograph shows what the inside of a slave quarters at Mount Vernon may have looked like.

~ Living in the Greenhouse Slave Quarters ~

Each room of the Greenhouse Slave Quarters had a single door to the outside and provided about 600 square feet (55 sq m) of living space. As many as 60 people may have lived in the quarters, so it's likely 15 lived in each room. It's believed the quarters were designed to house adults who didn't have families with them. Some also lived in rooms above the kitchen building, and families had individual cabins across from the greenhouse. The greenhouse and the attached quarters were destroyed by fire twice, in 1835 and again in 1863.

Enslaved people on Mount Vernon's other farms were farther away from Washington. This typically allowed for more privacy. They also usually lived in cabins meant to house either one family or two families in separate spaces. While the privacy may have been better, the quality of construction was much poorer than at the House for Families or the Greenhouse Slave Quarters.

These cabins were smeared with mud in an unsuccessful effort to keep out wind and rain. A cabin for one family had a single room and often a wooden chimney made of sticks plastered with mud on an outside wall. A cabin for two families had two rooms, each with its own entrance, separated by a chimney in the middle. The cabins had few windows and likely no glass in the windows they did have.

This photograph shows how the inside of an enslaved family's cabin may have looked at Mount Vernon.

~ A Visitor's Account ~

For the people living in the cabins, a single small room served as living room, kitchen, and bedroom. A man who once visited George Washington at Mount Vernon left an account of the inside of one of the cabins: "The husband and wife sleep on a mean pallet, the children on the ground; a very bad fireplace, some utensils for cooking, but in the middle of this poverty some cups and a teapot." He also described the conditions of the living quarters as "wretched," meaning they were of very poor quality.

Here, people are visiting a cabin made to look like one where enslaved workers on Mount Vernon would have lived. A family of eight would have lived in one like this.

17

clothing

While Washington supplied clothing for the people he enslaved, it was the least amount possible, plain, and often coarse. Most enslaved people received clothing annually, plus an additional item or two as necessary for the changing seasons. Since they received few items of clothing, they often wore the same clothes day after day.

Some clothing was made from cloth produced at Mount Vernon or imported cloth, while some was ordered ready-made in large quantities. Fabrics included wool and unbleached coarse linen called osnaburg. Washington complained when a seamstress made long pants for the men instead of short breeches because they used too much cloth. The poorest clothing

went to children and adults too old to work. One December, a man in charge on one of the farms reported that children had no clothes.

This image shows Washington on a horse. The man standing is likely one of Washington's enslaved workers.

This image gives you an idea what some of the clothing worn by enslaved women working inside the Washington home may have looked like. Their dresses were often similar in style to Martha's, although they were much simpler and made out of much cheaper fabrics.

~ House and Field Clothing ~

Enslaved individuals who worked in the mansion were given more clothing of better quality than those who worked in the fields. Males wore suits known as liveries that were modeled after the three-piece suits commonly worn by wealthy men of the time. Liveries were commonly made of fine wool in the colors of the enslaver's **coat of arms**. Elaborately woven lace decorated the edges. Females who worked in the house wore dresses made of fine cloth, with an apron of delicate linen called lawn.

Even when they weren't doing their jobs, the enslaved people at Mount Vernon were often working. The most important daily activities were housekeeping chores. Enslaved workers kept small gardens and raised chickens to add to the **rations** Washington provided them. They needed to tend the chickens and gardens, cook and preserve what they got from their gardens, and do what was necessary to care for their clothing, such as cleaning and mending.

The chickens, the eggs they laid, and the produce from the garden could provide the enslaved workers with income as well. They sometimes sold the food and goods they made at the Sunday market in Alexandria. Washington himself even purchased food from people he enslaved, as well as items such as brooms that they had made.

Enslaved people kept chicken coops like this one to raise chickens and produce eggs.

Laundry and cooking were also chores enslaved people needed to do when they were not performing their forced labor.

~ More Ways to Make Money ~

Some enslaved people at Mount Vernon earned money through fishing and hunting. Washington enjoyed fish and would pay good money for fine ones. Tom Davis and Sambo Anderson were two men Washington enslaved. They were well-known hunters and sold Washington 132 birds in the fall of 1792. When Anderson received his freedom after Washington's death, he supported himself by hunting wild game and selling it to hotels. Other enslaved people sold their teeth to dentists for use in **dentures** and in tooth transplant operations.

coffee and teas

Some enslaved workers at Mount Vernon, such as the Washingtons' chef Hercules, spent the money they earned on better clothing. Hercules was renowned for his cooking skill. He accompanied the Washingtons to Philadelphia, the nation's capital at the time, while Washington served as president. There, he earned up to $200 a year selling leftovers from the kitchen. This income allowed him to purchase fine white linen, a black silk waistcoat, a blue cloth coat with a velvet collar, and a gold-headed cane. This clothing was far superior to any of the clothes enslaved workers were given.

Others preferred to use money on good food. They purchased imported foods such as tea, coffee, molasses, and sugar from shops in Alexandria and fine flour and pork from Washington himself.

This is the dining room at Mount Vernon, where the Washingtons would have eaten meals prepared for them by Hercules.

~ Items for the Home ~

Some enslaved workers used the money they earned to purchase furniture and other items for their living quarters. Surviving legal documents provide a lengthy list of items one woman acquired for her home. That list includes a desk, three tables, eight chairs, two mirrors, 13 pictures, 18 plates, six teacups, a sugar dish, a cream pot, and two beds. For a wealthy free person of the time that probably wouldn't seem like much, but it's remarkable compared to the furnishings of the average quarters of an enslaved person.

Enslaved life was cruel, but the individuals were determined to create good times when they could. When they were not working and were done with their own housework and chores, they found ways to enjoy their free time. A favorite activity was visiting each other at night, after they had finished work for the day. Enslaved workers on the outer farms went from cabin to cabin to see each other. Washington complained they were too tired after what he called "night walking" to do the work he expected them to do.

Many also enjoyed swimming and playing games and sports. A visitor to Mount Vernon observed 30 enslaved people playing a team sport called "prisoner's base." The visitor noted they played the athletic game with great enthusiasm and energy.

This painting shows enslaved people dancing and playing music.

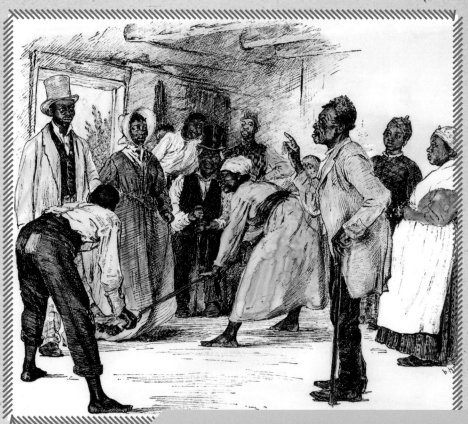

This image shows enslaved Black people taking part in a wedding ceremony known as "Jumping the Broom." Many Black people still take part in this tradition at weddings today.

~ Family Time ~

Down time often included spending time with family. However, some husbands and wives were separated because they worked on different farms at Mount Vernon. Others were married to people who lived on different plantations. These couples could only visit each other on days off–Sundays and holidays. And sometimes they couldn't even do that. Some enslavers forbade enslaved people from other plantations from coming to their plantation. When families could visit with each other, it often involved music and storytelling. Those who had been born in Africa told stories about life in that distant land.

Resisting Slavery

Enslaved people in America, including those at Mount Vernon, often resisted slavery. They did this by faking illness, working slowly, doing poor work, and misplacing or damaging tools and equipment. Anyone, regardless of age or state of health, could resist by these means. It was hard to prove they did these things on purpose, though some enslavers would punish them regardless.

Theft was another means of resistance. It was more dangerous because the offender was more likely to be caught and punished. Some were accused of stealing tools, fabrics, milk, butter, fruits, meats, corn, potatoes, and more. Washington himself detected a scheme to steal wool by claiming it was too dirty to spin: "I perceive [observe] by the Spinning Report of last week, that each of the spinners have deducted [removed] half a pound for dirty wool."

How Enslaved Workers Resisted

faking illness

misplacing or damaging equipment

working slowly

doing poor work

stealing

escaping

Enslavers, including Washington, may not have always known when some forms of resistance were occurring.

~ Making an Escape ~

By far, the greatest expression of resistance was escape. Seventeen enslaved individuals escaped Mount Vernon during the American Revolution when a British warship was anchored nearby. Supplies were offered to the ship in exchange for the individuals, but the captain refused to return them. It came as somewhat of a surprise to the Washingtons that house workers who were considered to have more privileged positions than others—Hercules, the chef, and Martha's personal maid, Oney (Ona) Judge—escaped. Of course, even the most "privileged" enslaved people were treated cruelly. It should come as no surprise they desired freedom.

Archaeologists have uncovered a lot of important history about slavery at Mount Vernon. In 2014, they began a project at the Slave **Cemetery**. It's especially important because so little is known about the cemetery. In fact, it was never mentioned during Washington's lifetime.

The earliest account comes from the journal of a woman who visited Mount Vernon in 1833, when the Washington family still owned it. She wrote that near Washington's tomb "you see the burying place of his slaves."

It's not known how many graves are in the burial ground. The 1833 account mentions 150 graves. An

IN MEMORY OF
THE AFRO AMERICANS
WHO SERVED AS SLAVES
AT MOUNT VERNON
THIS MONUMENT MARKING THEIR
BURIAL GROUND
DEDICATED
SEPTEMBER 21, 1983
MOUNT VERNON
LADIES' ASSOCIATION

account from 1838 says 100 graves. By 2017, the project had found and documented 70 graves, but archaeologists are still working on the site. Special care is taken to respect those buried and remember all who were enslaved at Washington's home.

You can visit Mount Vernon to learn more about its history of slavery. There, you can see this marker, which honors enslaved people who worked at Mount Vernon.

~ Marking the Graves ~

It's possible graves in the Slave Cemetery once had markers with names, but of the 70 burials documented by 2017, only one had what archaeologists believed may have been such a marker. It was not inscribed but stuck out prominently. It's possible that when the cemetery was in use, burial mounds were used to identify graves. Over time, they were weathered away and are no longer visible.

Even without markers, it's believed certain well-known enslaved workers were buried at the cemetery, including Washington's personal servant, William Lee.

GLOSSARY

artifact: something made by humans in the past

cemetery: a place where the dead are buried

chimney: a vertical structure that is part of a building and is designed to carry off the smoke from a fireplace

coat of arms: a design of symbols standing for a family, city, or country

contradiction: conflict, disagreement

denture: a set of false teeth

distiller: a person who produces alcoholic drinks through a process that involves heating liquids to concentrate them

document: a formal piece of writing

quarters: the housing occupied by a group

rations: a controlled amount of food given to a person

seamstress: a woman who sews by hand to make and repair clothes, curtains, and household linens

utensil: an item that is useful or necessary in a household, such as a spoon or a knife

FOR MORE INFORMATION

Books

Cooke, Tim. *George Washington*. New York, NY: Gareth Stevens Publishing, 2020.

Kawa, Katie. *Slavery Wasn't Only in the South: Exposing Myths About the Civil War*. New York, NY: Gareth Stevens Publishing, 2020.

Uhl, Xina M., and Tonya Buell. *A Primary Source Investigation of Slavery*. New York, NY: Rosen Central, 2019.

Websites

George Washington's Mount Vernon: Slavery
www.mountvernon.org/george-washington/slavery/
Find out more about slavery at Mount Vernon with biographies on some of the enslaved people, photographs of artifacts, and much more.

Mount Vernon, Virginia
www.nps.gov/nr/travel/presidents/mount_vernon.html
Read about the history of Mount Vernon and the Washington family on this website.

INDEX